MW00974523

For: _Deanna Vázquez_

I thank my God every time I remember you.

Philippians 1:3

From: _Mami Vázquez_

Thank You

Copyright 1999 by ZondervanPublishingHouse
ISBN 0-310-97921-8

Requests for information should be addressed to:

📖 ZondervanPublishingHouse
Mail Drop B20
Grand Rapids, Michigan 49530
http://www.zondervan.com

Senior editor: Gwen Ellis
Project editor: Pat Matuszak
Designer: Mark Veldheer
Cover illustration: Michael Ingle

Printed in Hong Kong

99 00 01 /HK/ 3 2 1

Thank
You

Zondervan*Gifts*

We have a gift for inspiration™

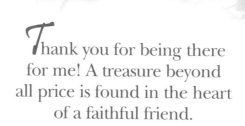

*T*hank you for being there
for me! A treasure beyond
all price is found in the heart
of a faithful friend.

Pat Matuszak

*P*erfume and incense bring joy
    to the heart,
and the pleasantness of one's
    friend springs from his
    earnest counsel.

Proverbs 27:9

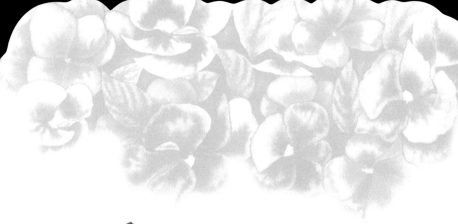

$\mathcal{S}$ome feelings are to mortals
given
With less of earth in them than
heaven.

Sir Walter Scott

*F*ollow my example, as I follow
the example of Christ.

1 Corinthians 11:1

*O*ne who knows how to show and
to accept kindness will be a friend
better than any possession.

Sophocles

*P*raise tests a person, just as high temperatures test metal. . .
People of high integrity are not swayed by praise. They are attuned to their inner convictions, and they do what they should whether or not they are praised.

NIV Life Application Bible

*T*o those who know thee not, no
words can paint!
And those who know thee, know all
words are faint!

Hannah Moore

$\mathcal{T}$he crucible for silver and the
furnace for gold,
but man is tested by the praise
he receives.

Proverbs 27:21

God has two dwellings; one
in heaven, and the other in
a thankful heart.

Isaac Walton

$\mathcal{I}$ thank my God through Jesus Christ for all of you.

Romans 1:8

I look upon every day to be lost, in which I do not make a new acquaintance.

Samuel Johnson

I always thank God for you
because of his grace given you
in Christ Jesus. For in him
you have been enriched in every
way —in all your speaking
and in all your knowledge.

1 Corinthians 1:4 –5

Gratitude is not only the memory
but the homage of
the heart rendered to God
for his goodness.

Nathaniel P. Willis

A friend loves at all times,
and a brother is born for
adversity.

Proverbs 17:17

A faithful friend is beyond price,
no sum can balance his worth.

Sirach

I thank my God every time I remember you. In all my prayers for all of you, I always pray with joy because of your partnership in the gospel from the first day until now.

Philippians 1:3 –5

$\mathcal{I}$ keep my friends as misers do their treasure, because, of all the things granted us by wisdom, none is greater or better than friendship.

Pietro Aretino

$\mathcal{G}$od is love. Whoever
lives in love lives in God,
and God in him.

1 John 4:16

$\mathcal{I}$f we would build on a sure
foundation in friendship, we
must love friends for their sake
rather than for our own.

Charlotte Brontë

The kingdom of heaven
is like a merchant looking
for fine pearls. When he
found one of great value, he went
away and sold everything he had
and bought it.

Matthew 13:45 –46

*F*riendship is Love
without his wings!

Lord Byron

$\mathcal{W}$e always thank God for
all of you, mentioning you in
our prayers. We continually
remember before our God and
Father your work produced by
faith, your labor prompted by love.

1 Thessalonians 1:2 – 3

$\mathcal{A}$ friend may well be
reckoned the masterpiece
of nature.

Ralph Waldo Emerson

$\mathcal{M}$ay the Lord direct your hearts into God's love and Christ's perseverance.

2 Thessalonians 3:5

We do not so much
need the help of our friends
as the confidence of their
help in need.

Epicurus

*W*e always thank God when we pray for you, because we have heard of your faith in Christ Jesus and of the love you have for all the saints —the faith and love that spring from the hope that is stored up for you in heaven.

Colossians 1:3–5

$\mathcal{F}$riendships begun in this world
will be taken up again, never to
be broken off.

Saint Francis de Sales

I thank God, whom I serve, . . .
as night and day I constantly
remember you in my prayers.
Recalling your tears, I long to see
you, so that I may be filled with joy.

2 Timothy 1:3 –4

*T*he friend in my adversity I shall always cherish most. I can better trust those who helped to relieve the gloom of my dark hours than those who are so ready to enjoy with me the sunshine of my prosperity.

Ulysses S. Grant

$\mathcal{L}$et the peace of Christ rule in
your hearts, since as members of
one body you were called to
peace. And be thankful.

Colossians 3:15

$\mathcal{F}$riendship is precious,
not only in the shade, but
in the sunshine of life.

Thomas Jefferson

God did not give us a spirit of
timidity, but a spirit of power, of
love and of self-discipline.

2 Timothy 1:7

$\mathcal{T}$rue friendship ought never to
conceal what it thinks.

Saint Jerome

$\mathcal{B}$etter is open rebuke
than hidden love.
Wounds from a friend can be
trusted.

Proverbs 27:5 –6

$\mathcal{T}$o let friendship die away
by negligence and silence
is certainly not wise. It is
voluntarily to throw away
one of the greatest comforts
of the weary pilgrimage.

Samuel Johnson

$\mathcal{I}$always thank my God as I remember you in my prayers, because I hear about your faith in the Lord Jesus and your love for all the saints.

Philemon 4 –5

$\mathcal{A}$ true friend is the greatest of all blessings, and that which we take the least care to acquire.

François duc de La Rochefoucauld

$\mathcal{T}$he wise in heart are called
discerning.

Proverbs 16:21

I desire to so conduct the affairs of
this administration that if at the end,
when I come to lay down the reins
of power, I have lost every other
friend on earth, I shall at least have
one friend left, and that friend shall
be down inside of me.

Abraham Lincoln

Night and day we pray most
earnestly that we may see you again.

1 Thessalonians 3:10

*T*hank you for memories of times
we spent together.

Pat Matuszak

*B*e slow to fall into friendship;
but when thou art in, continue
firm and constant.

Socrates

Every word of God is flawless;
he is a shield to those who take
refuge in him.

Proverbs 30:5

$\mathcal{M}$ay your right hand always be stretched out in friendship, but never in want.

Irish toast

The Spirit of the Sovereign LORD is
    on me, . . .
He has sent me to bind up the
    brokenhearted, . . .
    to comfort all who mourn, . . .
They will be called oaks of
    righteousness,
    a planting of the LORD.

Isaiah 61:1 –3

*I*f you want to be happy for a
year, plant a garden; if you want to
be happy for life, plant a tree.

English proverb

*I*t is right for me to feel this way about all of you, since I have you in my heart.

Philippians 1:7

$\mathcal{T}$hose who reach out to clasp a hand with loving hearts change the world.

Pat Matuszak

$\mathcal{W}$e know that in all things
God works for the good of those
who love him.

Romans 8:28

$\mathcal{F}$riends are as companions on
a journey, who ought to aid
each other to persevere in
the road to a happier life.

Pythagoras

*Y*our love has given me great
joy and encouragement.

Philemon 7

Our Lord does not care so much for the importance of our works as for the love with which they are done.

Saint Teresa of Avila

*I*f you spend yourselves . . .
then your light will rise in the
darkness.

Isaiah 58:10

The friend who can be silent with us in a moment of despair or confusion, who can stay with us in an hour of grief and bereavement, who can tolerate not knowing, not curing, not healing and face with us the reality of our powerlessness, that is a friend who cares.

Henri Nouwen

*K*eep me safe, O God,
for in you I take refuge. I said to
the LORD, "You are my Lord;
apart from you I have no good
thing." As for the saints who
are in the land,
they are the glorious ones in
whom is all my delight.

Psalm 16:1 –3

$\mathcal{I}$t is only true friends who will
tell you when your face is dirty.

Italian proverb

$\mathcal{M}$ay the Lord make your love
increase and overflow for each
other and for everyone else, just
as ours does for you.

1 Thessalonians 3:12

*H*e who fears God behaves
accordingly, and his friend
will be like himself.

Sirach

LORD, who may dwell in your
    sanctuary?
Who may live on your holy hill?
    He whose walk is blameless
and who does what is righteous,
who speaks the truth from his
    heart
and has no slander on his tongue,
who does his neighbor no wrong.

Psalm 15:1 –3

$\mathcal{W}$e live in an ascending scale
when we live happily,
one thing leading to another
in an endless series.

Robert Louis Stevenson

Commit to the LORD whatever you do, and your plans will succeed.

Proverbs 16:3

$\mathscr{W}$hen you have once seen the glow of happiness on the face of a beloved person, you know that a man can have no vocation but to awaken that light on the faces surrounding him.

Albert Camus

$\mathcal{W}$e are God's workmanship,
created in Christ Jesus to do good
works, which God prepared in
advance for us to do.

Ephesians 2:10

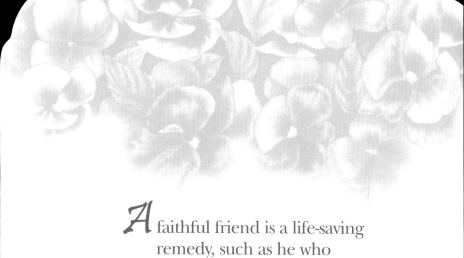

A faithful friend is a life-saving
remedy, such as he who
fears God finds.

Sirach

$\mathcal{W}$e know, brothers loved by God, that he has chosen you, because our gospel came to you not simply with words, but also with power, with the Holy Spirit and with deep conviction.

1 Thessalonians 1:4 –5

$\mathcal{E}$lectronic communication will never be a substitute for the face of someone who with their soul encourages another person to be brave and true.

Charles Dickens

$\mathcal{J}$ust as you received Christ Jesus
as Lord, continue to live in him,
rooted and built up in him,
strengthened in the faith as you
were taught.

Colossians 2:6 –7

I believe that any man's life will be filled with constant and unexpected encouragement, if he makes up his mind to do his level best each day, and as nearly as possible reaching the high water mark of pure and useful living.

Booker T. Washington

*D*ear friends, since God so
loved us, we also ought to love
one another.

1 John 4:11

A kind mouth multiplies
friends, and gracious lips
prompt friendly greetings.

Sirach

$\mathcal{L}$et us not become weary in doing good, for at the proper time we will reap a harvest if we do not give up.

Galatians 6:9

Kind words toward those you
daily meet,
Kind words and actions right,
Will make this life of ours most
sweet,
Turn darkness into light.

Isaac Watts

*B*e rich in good deeds.
Be generous and willing
to share. Take hold of
the life that is truly life.

1 Timothy 6:18 –19

No one is rich enough to do
without a neighbor.

Folk proverb

*P*raise the LORD, all you nations;
   extol him, all you peoples.
For great is his love toward us,
   and the faithfulness of the LORD
   endures forever.

Psalm 117:1–2

No people on earth have more cause to be thankful than ours, and this is said reverently, with gratitude to the Giver of Good who has blessed us with the conditions which have enabled us to achieve so large a measure of well-being and of happiness.

Theodore Roosevelt

*H*ow can we thank God
enough for you in return for all
the joy we have in the presence
of our God because of you?

1 Thessalonians 3:9

$\mathcal{B}$eggar that I am, I am
even poor in thanks.

Shakespeare

$\mathcal{W}$e also thank God continually because, when you received the word of God, which you heard from us, you accepted it not as the word of men, but as it actually is, the word of God, which is at work in you who believe.

1 Thessalonians 2:13

$\mathcal{T}$hank you for your words that
help me hear God's voice in my
life.

Pat Matuszak

$\mathcal{D}$ear children, let us not love
with words or tongue but with
actions and in truth. This then is
how we know that we belong to
the truth, and how we set our
hearts at rest in his presence.

1 John 3:18 –19

$\mathcal{H}$appiness is not a goal;
it is a by-product.

Eleanor Roosevelt

$\mathcal{T}$wo are better than one . . .
If one falls down,
    his friend can help him up . . .
Though one may be
    overpowered,
    two can defend themselves.

Ecclesiastes 4:9–10,12

Strengthening one another
with the true hope Jesus offers
is one of the most important
things we can do. We can do
this in many little ways that
make a difference.

Jan Dravecky

*T*his is how we know what love
is: Jesus Christ laid down his life
for us. And we ought to lay down
our lives for our brothers.

1 John 3:16

$\mathcal{T}$he true secret of giving
advice is, after you have
honestly given it, to be perfectly
indifferent whether it is taken
or not, and never persist in
trying to set people right.

Hannah Whitall Smith

Surely goodness and love will
follow me all the days of my life.

Psalm 23:6

One word frees us of all
the weight and pain of
life; that word is love.

Sophocles

*I*mitate those who through
faith and patience inherit
what has been promised.

Hebrews 6:12

Successful people apply to
their own lives the same advice
they prescribe for others.

Anonymous

$\mathcal{T}$he wisdom that comes from heaven is first of all pure; then peace-loving, considerate, submissive, full of mercy and good fruit, impartial and sincere.

James 3:17

$\mathcal{S}$ow good services:
sweet remembrances
will grow from them.

Germaine de Stael

$\mathcal{L}$et the word of Christ dwell in you richly as you teach and admonish one another with all wisdom, and as you sing psalms, hymns and spiritual songs with gratitude in your hearts to God.

Colossians 3:16

$\mathcal{W}$e only consult the ear
because the heart is waiting.

Blaise Pascal

$\mathcal{D}$ear friends, let us love
one another, for love comes
from God. Everyone who
loves has been born of
God and knows God.

1 John 4:7

*T*rue love's the gift which God
    has given
It is the secret sympathy,
The silver link, the silken tie,
Which heart to heart and mind to
    mind
In body and in soul can bind.

Sir Walter Scott

$\mathcal{I}$f anything is excellent
or praiseworthy — think
about such things.

Philippians 4:8

$\mathcal{L}$ife must be lived and
curiosity kept alive. One
must never, for whatever
reason, turn his back on life.

Eleanor Roosevelt

$\mathcal{T}$he Lord will guide you always;
he will satisfy your needs in a
sun-scorched land . . .
You will be like a well-watered
garden.

Isaiah 58:11

$\mathcal{T}$o love is to give one's time. We never give the impression that we care when we are in a hurry.

Paul Tournier

$\mathcal{N}$ow we see but a poor reflection as in a mirror; then we shall see face to face. Now I know in part; then I shall know fully, even as I am fully known.

1 Corinthians 13:12

*T*here are people who in spite
of their merit disgust us,
and others who please us in
spite of their faults.

François duc de La Rochefoucauld

May the Lord strengthen your hearts so that you will be blameless and holy in the presence of our God and Father when our Lord Jesus comes with all his holy ones.

1 Thessalonians 3:13

*H*ave a heart that never hardens, and a temper that never tires, and a touch that never hurts.

Charles Dickens

$\mathcal{J}$esus said, "Whoever drinks the water I give him will never thirst. Indeed, the water I give him will become in him a spring of water welling up to eternal life."

John 4:14

$\mathcal{T}$he greatest good you can
do for another is not just to
share your riches, but to
reveal to him his own.

Benjamin Disraeli

We constantly pray for you,
that our God may count you
worthy of his calling, and that by
his power he may fulfill every
good purpose of yours and every
act prompted by your faith.

2 Thessalonians 1:11

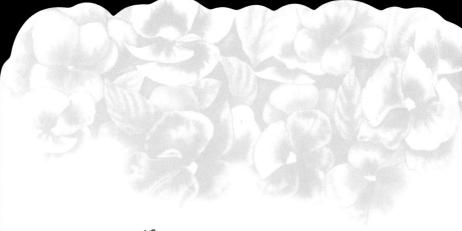

$\mathcal{T}$he word *trust* is the heart of faith. Trust sees and feels, and it leans on those who have a great, living, and genuine heart of love.

Mrs. Charles Cowman

$\mathcal{K}$eep on loving each other.

Hebrews 13:1

$\mathcal{W}$e find rest in those we love,
and we provide a resting place in
ourselves for those who love us.

Bernard of Clairvaux

$\mathcal{N}$either death nor life, . . .
nor anything else in all creation,
will be able to separate us
from the love of God that is
in Christ Jesus our Lord.

Romans 8:38 –39

*T*he rose is fairest when't is
budding new,
And hope is brightest when it
dawns from fears.
The rose is sweetest wash'd with
morning dew,
And love is loveliest when
embalm'd in tears.

Sir Walter Scott

*E*very good and perfect gift is
from above, coming down from
the Father of the heavenly lights.

James 1:17

$\mathcal{T}$hy love is such I can no way
repay;
The heavens reward thee
manifold, I pray.

Anne Bradstreet

$\mathcal{W}$e ought always to thank God
for you, brothers, and rightly so,
because your faith is growing
more and more, and the love
every one of you has for each
other is increasing.

2 Thessalonians 1:3

*L*ife without thankfulness is lacking in fine perception. Faith without thankfulness lacks strength and fortitude. Every virtue divorced from thankfulness is maimed and limps along the spiritual road.

John Henry Jowett

Live a life of love, just as
Christ loved us and gave
himself up for us.

Ephesians 5:2

$\mathcal{I}$n love, there is always one
who kisses and one who
offers the cheek.

French proverb

$\mathcal{L}$et everything that has breath
praise the LORD.

Psalm 150:6

The unthankful heart . . . discovers no mercies; but the thankful heart . . . will find, in every hour, some heavenly blessings.

Henry Ward Beecher

*L*et love and faithfulness never
    leave you; . . .
    write them on the tablet of
    your heart.
Then you will win favor and a
    good name
    in the sight of God and man.
Trust in the LORD with all your
    heart.

Proverbs 3:3 –5

$\mathcal{W}$rite your injuries in dust,
your benefits in marble.

Benjamin Franklin

*G*od can testify how I long for all of you with the affection of Christ Jesus. And this is my prayer: that your love may abound more and more in knowledge and depth of insight.

Philippians 1:8 –9

$\mathcal{T}$hank you for being so
generous with your time.

Pat Matuszak

He who began a good work in
you will carry it on to completion
until the day of Christ Jesus.

Philippians 1:6

Sources

NIV Christian Growth Study Bible (Grand Rapids: Zondervan, 1997).

NIV Life Application Bible (Grand Rapids: Zondervan, 1991).

Jan Dravecky, *Stand by Me* (Grand Rapids: Zondervan, 1998).